TWELVE WALKS

INTRODUCTION

This is the third edition of a booklet designed to help walkers enjoy the outstanding natural beauty in the area covered by the OTTER VALLEY ASSOCIATION. Twelve walks are described, up the valley as far as Harpford and Venn Ottery, to the East along the hilltop boundary with the neighbouring Sid Vale Association, and to the West along the cliffs to West Down Beacon then inland over the Commons of East Budleigh, Bicton and Colaton Raleigh, where there is an overlap with the Exmouth Society's area. A map of the area showing the starting places of the walks is given on pages 10–11. Each walk is described on a page faced by a diagram.

Several of the walks give extensive views of the coastline of Lyme Bay from Portland Bill to Berry Head. The ground covered includes clifftops, hills and vales, woods and commons, and rich agricultural land. There are villages of historical interest and charm, a brief history of which, together with that of Budleigh Salterton, is covered by another book – *The Lower Otter Valley* – published by the Otter Valley Association. Above all there is the river Otter meandering through water meadows and marshes to the Saltings, which give their name to Budleigh Salterton. Coleridge wrote of "Lovely Otter's sleep persuading stream". By the water's edge the peace and stillness is pierced only by the cry of birds. The seasons, time of day, clouds and tides bring ever-changing light and colours.

The red sandstone cliffs with their famous pebble-beds are best seen from the sea when the sun is low, casting sharp shadows on the sculptured relief. A second best is the view from Budleigh Salterton War Memorial, at sunrise looking West.

Budleigh Salterton has grown from a tiny hamlet of fishermen's cottages near the South Parade, most of it within the last 150 years, but there are some fine Regency houses in East Terrace, and the early 19th-century thatched Fairlynch, now a Museum and Arts Centre, is a must for the visitor.

East Budleigh and Otterton are both older and mentioned in the Domesday Survey. Until recently each was larger than Budleigh Salterton. Local people will tell you that "Budleigh" means East Budleigh and that Budleigh Salterton, which only became a parish in 1900, should be called plain "Salterton".

East of Budleigh Salterton's Marine Parade is one of the limekilns which used to be a feature of Devon, where limestone was brought by sea and converted to quicklime. It is not known when this kiln was last in use, but children still played in the ruined ovens in the early 1930s, before the ovens were finally filled in and bricked up.

From the lime kiln a pebble bank runs East, almost closing the mouth of the Otter, so that the estuary has silted up. There are conflicting reports about when the river ceased to be navigable. According to one report, it could be used by 60-ton vessels as late as 1810. Major movements have occurred quite recently: the pebble bank is said to have doubled its width between 1808 and 1863. In the 15th century, Budleigh (Budley) Haven on the west bank was a thriving port for East Budleigh and Otterton was a fishing village where sea-going vessels could berth.

When the embankment was built by French prisoners of war (said to have been housed in the stables at Bicton), the river changed its course and lost its large loop at Kersbrook. The changing flow of tides up the English Channel continues to alter the beach. Storms in the 1960s threatened to breach the pebble bank and the local Council have reinforced it with gabions – wire cages filled with pebbles.

The area is fortunate to have so many footpaths. They are YOURS and you are urged to use them and so maintain public rights of way.

Most of the walks described are about five miles long. Some can be shortened, as indicated. More energetic walkers can combine two walks into a full day's outing, and the last walk is intended as a full day excursion. The recommended Ordnance Survey maps are the 1:25,000 sheets SY 08/18 (Sidmouth) and SY 09/19 (Ottery St. Mary). A few minor official diversions, which benefit all parties, have been made on short sections of one or two public paths marked on these maps. Where these occur, suitable waymarking should appear. You are advised to use the descriptions and sketches given here.

Places of special interest are marked with an asterisk (∗) in the text and are described on pages 4–8. Where old names of lanes are given on 1906 Ordnance Survey maps, but are now neither sign-posted nor given on the 1:25,000 maps, they are marked in the text "known as". The object is to revive the use of some of these old names.

Regular walkers might like to 'adopt' a footpath and keep it clear by occasional trimming with secateurs or billhooks.

Please help to preserve the goodwill of farmers and residents by following the Country Code, summarised on page 36. On page 9 is a list of recommended car parks from which the walks start.

Please park your car tidily. GOOD WALKING!

PLACES OF INTEREST
(Marked * in text)

* THE AMENITY WALK (Walk 2). Sponsored and developed by the Budleigh Salterton Town Council, a section of the disused railway track now provides a splendid ¾ mile of traffic-free walking for all to enjoy.

* THE AQUADUCT (Walk 2) leads water from Budleigh Brook (which runs through the village of East Budleigh) into the Otter; it was built to help drain the water-meadows and reclaim land for agriculture. Before the railway was built in 1897, the brook ran south, to the west of the Otter. Land reclamation and building of the embankment dates back to about 1815.

* ANCHORING HILL (Walks 6 and 7) is said to have provided a landmark to mariners using the river and anchorage at Otterton. The river was navigable to this point up to about 1450. One of the pew-ends of East Budleigh Church (see below) shows the type of boat used – a carrack – a small craft not needing deep water.

* BICTON CHURCHES (Walk 6). Of the older of the two, only the 12th century tower remains, together with ruined traceries of the 15th century. Adjoining it is a Mausoleum, designed by Pugin (1850): it contains the Rolle family vault. The newer church, by Hayward, was built by Lady Rolle in 1851 in memory of her husband, John, Lord Rolle (died in 1849). Dedicated to the Blessed Virgin Mary, its exterior is decorated with a series of carved heads representing the kings and queens of England from Edward I to Queen Victoria.

* BICTON PARK (Walk 6). Extensive Italianate 18th century gardens with tropical and cactus houses; the designs are said to based on André le Notre's gardens at Versailles. The famous Pinetum was planted in 1830, and contains some of the largest and finest specimens of conifers in England. Other attractions include a steam-operated Woodland Railway, a Countryside Museum and a restaurant. The park is open to the public from April to October and winter weekends.

Bicton House, north of the gardens, was erected in about 1730 on the site of an older mansion. Formerly the home of the Rolle and Clinton families, it was bought in 1957 by the Devon County Council and is now used as a College of Agriculture.

The frontage of the house is pleasing, and the gardens and ornamental lake is of great beauty. Note the avenue of huge monkey-puzzle trees.

* COLATON RALEIGH CHURCH St. John the Baptist's (Walks 7 & 8). Originally built before 1226, and rebuilt in 1875. The tower was rebuilt in the 15th century, but masonry at the base may be older. Part of the font is Norman. Wall painting is medieval Italian sgraffito plastering, revived by Richard Fulford, son of the then Vicar of Woodbury, when the Church was rebuilt in the 1870's.

* EAST BUDLEIGH (Walks 5 and 6). A typical East Devon village with thatched cottages and cob walls. Many new houses have been added, but the main street has been little altered. In the past it was an important centre when Budleigh Salterton was a tiny hamlet. It was entered in Domesday Book as Bodelie. The population then was probably in the order of 200–250, perhaps tilling some 800 acres of arable land. During the Middle Ages the wool trade flourished and there was a small port at Budley Haven from where wool was exported to southern Europe (see Kersbrook Cottages).

* EAST BUDLEIGH CHURCH All Saints' (Walks 5 and 6). An exceptionally fine church, largely 15th century and built on a lofty eminence overlooking the village. The list of Vicars goes back to Stephen, 1261. Sir Walter Raleigh's father was churchwarden here in 1561, and the Raleigh pew (1537) is the first on the north side of the nave. There is much of interest to be seen in the church, including many carved bench-ends of the early 16th century. An illustrated guide book can be bought in the church.

All Saints' was the parish church for Budleigh Salterton up to 1900. St. Peter's in Budleigh Salterton, was designed by G. H. Fellowes Prynne, and endowed by the Rolle family. It was consecrated in 1893 as a Chapel of Ease, and became the parish church for Budleigh Salterton seven years later.

* FAIRLYNCH (Walk 2). A delightful thatched cottage orné, built in 1811 and converted in 1967 into a Museum and Arts Centre. It houses a geological collection and a local history room. Two large rooms are used for changing exhibitions, mostly of Victoriana and costumes; local arts and crafts are also shown for short periods. An exceptional archive of material covering every aspect of local life is available during opening hours, or by appointment with the librarian.

* HARPFORD CHURCH St. Gregory's (Walk 11) was almost entirely rebuilt in 1884. The Rev. Toplady (see Venn Ottery, p. 8) was Vicar of this church in 1766. The old churchyard cross was restored in his memory in 1913.

✻ HAYES BARTON (Walk 5). Sir Walter Raleigh was born in this house in 1552. Built in the 12th century, it was later restored in an E-shape, this being the practice of the time as a compliment to Queen Elizabeth I. The house was acquired by Richard Duke (see p. 7) about 1540. In 1584 Sir Walter Raleigh tried, unsuccessfully, to buy it from him. At the end of the 18th century the house became part of the Rolle Estate (now the Clinton Devon Estates). It is still used as a farmhouse.

✻ HAYES WOOD (Walk 4). A beautiful stretch of ancient dedicated woodland known to have been in existence since before 1400.

✻ KEBLE'S SEAT (Walk 12). Named after John Keble, noted theologian and founder of Keble College, Oxford. Keble often rested here, as did Alfred Lord Tennyson.

✻ KERSBROOK (Walk 2). Said to be a hybrid word, meaning the brook from the camp (Welsh, caer; Latin, castra). It drains the valley behind Tidwell House (see p. 8).

✻ KERSBROOK COTTAGES (Walk 2) are probably built on the site of the little medieval port of Budleigh or Budley Haven (see East Budleigh). The Haven's activity declined after about 1450 when the Otter ceased to be navigable for sea-going ships owing to the growth of the pebble bank across its mouth. However, flatbottomed boats were able to reach Bankly Wharf, about half a mile upstream, until the late 18th century (cf. Anchoring Hill).

✻ LITTLEHAM CHURCH (Walk 3). Dedicated to St. Margaret with St. Andrew, this was the parish church for Exmouth. The Chancel, the oldest part of the present structure, was built in the early 13th century. One of the windows in the north aisle contains 15th century glass. On the east wall of the Chantry Chapel is a memorial to Lady Nelson (1831) who is buried in the churchyard with her son, Josiah Nisbet.

✻ MONKS' WALK (Walk 12). The monks from Otterton Priory are said to have used this track (also known as Bar's Lane) to walk to their Chapel of Ease at Sidmouth.

✻ NEWTON POPPLEFORD CHURCH (Walks 10 and 11). St. Luke's used to be a Chapel of Ease for Aylesbeare Church. The tower and porch are 13th century; the bulk of the present church was built in 1897.

✻ NORTHMOSTOWN (Walk 12) derived from Northmost-tun, the most northerly farm in the parish of Otterton.

∗ OBELISK (Walk 6) was erected south of Bicton Gardens in 1730 as a "point de vue".

∗ THE OCTAGON (Walk 2). A quaint, eight-sided house, built in the early 19th century; it still belongs to the descendants of the first owner. Sir John Millais painted his well-known picture "The Boyhood of Raleigh" in this building, which he rented in 1869–70. For models, Millais used his sons Everett and George, and an old sailor named Vincent who was employed working a ferry across the Otter.

∗ OTTERTON (Walks 2, 6, 7 and 12). The Village appears in the Domesday Book as Otritone (later changed to Auterton and Autre). It was probably founded soon after the Anglo-Saxons invaded Devon in the 7th century. The Manor of Otterton belonged to Githa (or Gwytha), mother of Harold the last Saxon King, who was killed in the Battle of Hastings, 1066. The village then supported 5 villein farmers, 33 saltmakers and their families, and there were three mills. The property was granted to the Benedictine Abbey of Mont St. Michel in Normandy. Otterton Priory, close to the present church, was founded in the time of William II. The Prior was excommunicated in 1387. In 1414, Henry V founded Syon Abbey at Isleworth, and Otterton was given over to Syon until the dissolution of the monasteries by Henry VIII (1539).
In 1540, Richard Duke, then Clerk to the Court of Augmentation, bought Otterton and other neighbouring properties for £1,727. Part of the monastic buildings was converted into a mansion. Below the present church, you can see what survives of the old dwelling; it is now four council houses. Note the armorial bearings over the porch. Otterton village is very picturesque with several houses dating from the 17th and 18th centuries, mostly of cob and thatch. In the 14th century Otterton was easily the largest village in the whole area. As late as 1860, the population was said to be 1,245; by 1947 it had shrunk to 560.
Near the bridge is Otterton Mill, listed in Domesday, recently restored, and still working. It now houses craft workshops, exhibitions and a restaurant. The main street of Otterton is a Conservation Area.

∗ OTTERTON CHURCH (Walk 2). Dedicated to St. Michael and all Angels, the church was rebuilt in 1871 by Lady Rolle; only the red sandstone tower (at the east and not west end) remains of the ancient structure. The ancient Priory had a choir extending to the east of the tower: see markings on the tower base. The tower used to be flat-topped, like those of neighbouring churches: the pyramidal spire was added later. The church contains an old font and memorials to the Duke family.

✻ OTTERTON PARK (Walks 1 and 2). About 1775 the property of the Duke family was offered for sale after the death of the last heir. The description included "A park with 150 deer". The last heir is said to have planned a new mansion: this was never built, but some 200 year old trees survive. There are no deer in the park now. The property was finally bought, together with Hayes Barton and Poer Hayes, by Dennys Rolle of North Devon in 1785 for £72,000.

✻ PLACE COURT Colaton Raleigh (Walk 8) formerly belonged to the Abbots of Dunkeswell. The oldest part was built in the 13th century. It became the Dean's House when Parish and Revenues were given to the first Dean of Exeter, who was the first recorded vicar of Colaton Raleigh. There is a chapel over the porch, where Sir Walter Raleigh is said to have been baptised.

✻ TIDWELL HOUSE (Walk 4). The present building (1730) stands on the site of a much older manor which used to belong to the St. Clere family. It was bought by Lord Rolle in 1832 for £10,000. It is now a hotel.

✻ VENN OTTERY CHURCH St. Gregory's (Walk 10) contains fine carved pew-ends. The Saxon tower dates back to about 1095. Note the old door on the west side. Much of the remainder of the church was destroyed by fire in 1790. The nave was rebuilt in 1882. The author of "Rock of Ages", the Rev. A. M. Toplady (1740–1778) was vicar for a time. Venn Ottery is mentioned in the Domesday Book (Venn = fen: it appears as Fenotri in 1158 records).

✻ VICAR'S MEAD (Walk 5). A splendidly thatched 15th century private house with a high wall, also thatched, at one time the vicarage of East Budleigh. It is said that Sir Walter Raleigh received his early schooling here from the vicar. The house, with its hiding places, carries many legends associated with smuggling in the old days.

✻ WEST DOWN BEACON (Walk 3). "During the late Continental War", wrote William Baker in 1845, "a telegraphic station was fixed here, forming one of a chain between Start Point . . . and the Metropolis, by which intelligence could be transmitted throughout the whole distance in eighteen minutes".

✻ WOODBURY CASTLE (Walk 9). A prehistoric hill fort dating from about 1000 B.C. Of the surrounding ramparts four can still be seen clearly while parts of a fifth also remain.

WHERE TO START – CAR PARKS

BUDLEIGH SALTERTON;
(1) Lime Kiln Car Park, at east end of pebble beach.
    Approached from War Memorial at end of Marine Parade and
    Coastguards Road.
(2) White Bridge (for shortened version of Walk 1).
    At east end of South Farm Road, on north outskirts of town
    (going east from B3178)
(3) Public Hall, Station Road, 150 yards north of traffic lights.
    Free car park up the slope beside The Public Hall.

EAST BUDLEIGH; Below the church, off Hayes Lane.
Additional car parking at top of Vicarage Road.

EAST BUDLEIGH COMMON; (Squabmoor Reservoir).
(Grid reference 038 844). Where St. John's Road (which leaves
Exmouth towards the north-east) crosses the B3179 continue
north-east. In about $\frac{1}{4}$ mile the road bends sharp left and goes
steeply uphill for about 100 yards.
The car park is at the top of this slope, on the right.

OTTERTON; Parking on Fore Street by The Green.
Drive over the bridge, past the Mill and park on left.

COLATON RALEIGH; In Church Road (which runs east from
B3178 near Otter Inn): alongside the church or at the far end of
Church Road. Both places provide only limited parking.

NEWTON POPPLEFORD; At rear of church, off School Lane.

PEAK HILL (Muttersmoor). From Sidmouth follow the continuation
of the front westward, to the highest point; or along Ottery Road from
Otterton, right after $1\frac{1}{4}$ miles at Pinn Lane Corner, then further
$1\frac{1}{2}$ miles to the highest point.

STOWFORD; (Grid reference 056 866). From Yettington take the
road northwards alongside house called "Lufflands". Left at the first
crossroads. After about 300 yards park on left under trees.

BY "BUS"; Some of the starting points (including all those in
villages) can be reached by bus. For Information telephone
Stagecoach (0,1392) 427711 or (01395) 272395.

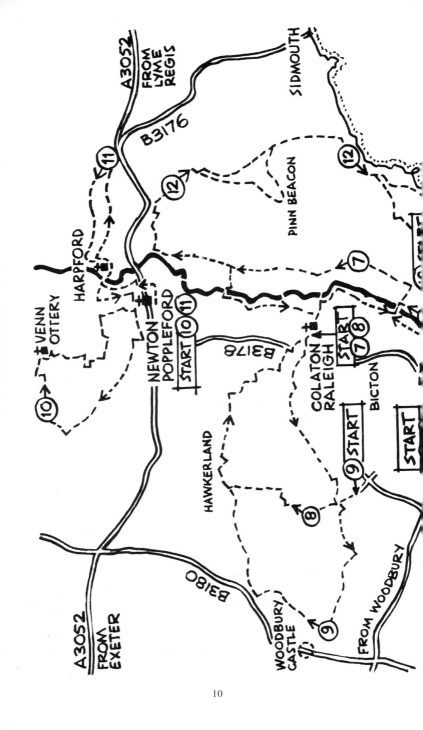

10

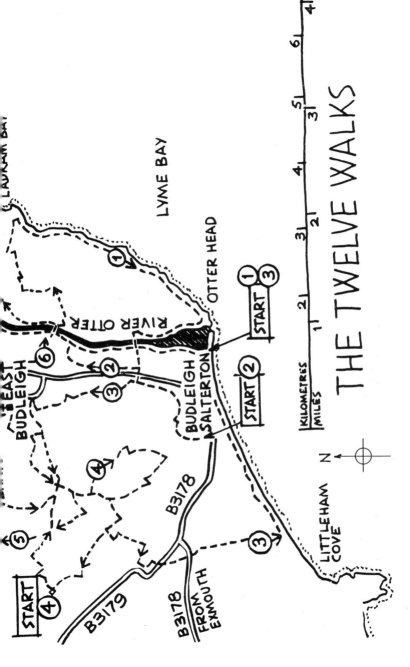

THE TWELVE WALKS

LYME BAY

LADRAM BAY

OTTER HEAD

RIVER OTTER

EAST BUDLEIGH

BUDLEIGH SALTERTON

LITTLEHAM COVE

START ① ③
START ②
START ④
START

B3178
B3179
B3178 FROM EXMOUTH

① ② ③ ④ ⑤ ⑥

N

KILOMETRES
MILES

11

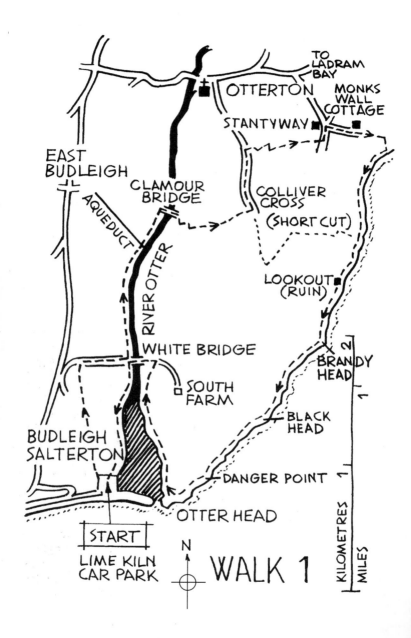

TO LADRAM BAY

OTTERTON

MONKS WALL COTTAGE

STANTYWAY

EAST BUDLEIGH

CLAMOUR BRIDGE

COLLIVER CROSS

(SHORT CUT)

AQUEDUCT

RIVER OTTER

LOOKOUT
(RUIN)

WHITE BRIDGE

SOUTH FARM

BRANDY HEAD

2

1

BUDLEIGH SALTERTON

BLACK HEAD

DANGER POINT

1

OTTER HEAD

START

LIME KILN CAR PARK

N

WALK 1

KILOMETRES

MILES

12

1.

Budleigh Salterton; Clamour Bridge; Colliver Cross; Stantyway; Ladram Bay; White Bridge; Budleigh Salterton

A river, country and coastal path walk of 6½ miles, which can be shortened to 5 miles by starting at and returning to White Bridge, and/or using the permissive path from Colliver Cross.

Leave the Lime Kiln Car Park at the North-West corner, behind SWW Pump House, pass through a kissing-gate along a track for a few yards, then turn right following footpath sign 'White Bridge 1 mile' along the left-hand side of a stream. After about ½ mile, turn right along the tarred road to White Bridge.

Immediately before the bridge turn left and follow the west bank of the river for almost a mile. Cross the first footbridge (Clamour Bridge). On tarred road turn sharp left and, just past two red brick columns of Otterton Park * sharp right through a gate to a footpath in a depression between hedges to another gate on left. Through this gate and following around the edge of the field to a small "pound". Take left exit (known as Colliver Lane). Continue 500 yards east between hedges to farm buildings (Colliver Cross).

For a shorter walk, turn right. Follow the tarred road to track which turns left and left again to meet another tarred road. Turn right over a stile onto the permissive path (marked "Private Road") continue past the sewage works, then turn immediately left, then right over a stile and straight onto the cliffs at Chiselbury Bay.

Turn left at Colliver Cross on tarred road. At top of rise, in sight of farm buildings, take lane on your right, then keep straight ahead bearing slightly right and then left to reach tarred road (Stantyway). Turn left and in a few yards, with a large barn on your left, and where the road divides, turn right (No Through Road) and fork right past Monks Wall Cottage onto a short footpath to a field overlooking Ladram Bay with magnificent view over Lyme Bay. Keep close to hedge on right until you reach cliff path. (Refreshments are available at the caravan park during the season, to get there take coastal path downhill to the left).

Turn right onto coast path past Chiselbury Bay, Brandy Head, Black Head and Danger Point to the estuary of the Otter; bear right here and keep to the field path hugging the fence/hedge on the left all the way up to the farm gate by South Farm Cottages, and out onto the road to White Bridge. Cross the bridge and turn immediately left by a gate onto the footpath leading back to the Lime Kiln Car Park.

* *See places of interest p. 4–8*

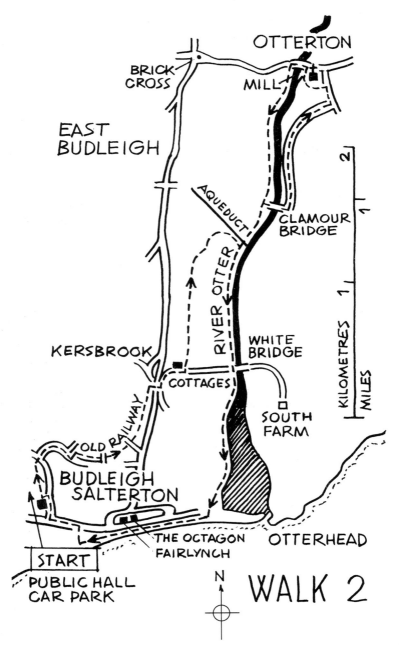

OTTERTON

BRICK CROSS

MILL

EAST BUDLEIGH

AQUEDUCT

CLAMOUR BRIDGE

RIVER OTTER

2

1

1

KILOMETRES

MILES

KERSBROOK

WHITE BRIDGE

COTTAGES

SOUTH FARM

OLD RAILWAY

BUDLEIGH SALTERTON

THE OCTAGON
FAIRLYNCH

OTTERHEAD

START

PUBLIC HALL
CAR PARK

N

WALK 2

14

2. Budleigh Salterton; Kersbrook; Clamour Bridge; Otterton; River Otter; Budleigh Salterton

Probably the most popular walk in the district, a distance of 5 miles which can be shortened to 3½ miles by turning right where the route first meets the river, and so back to the start via White Bridge.

Start from Public Hall car park; along the edge of the Green to join Station Road. Follow round the bend of the road (much safer on the inner curve pavement). Immediately after the road bridge over the disused railway (Leas Road), enter a gateway on the left and descend a slope leading to the old track, now transformed into an Amenity Walk *. This trail ends at Kersbrook *; down a flight of steps to the main road. Cross over and turn into South Farm Road, which lies parallel to the main road. This soon turns sharp right past three cottages (Kersbrook Cottages *). Just past a red cliff, turn left over a stile to footpath along the embankment with the extensive flood-plain to your right (sometimes muddy!). Continue for ⅔ mile on this path which bears right towards the end (waymarked), and runs parallel to the aqueduct * of the Budleigh brook to arrive at the Otter.

(At this point the walk can be shortened by 1½ miles: turn right, and follow river downstream to Lime Kiln car park. Then back to Public Hall as described below).

Otherwise keep left along the river path and cross footbridge (Clamour Bridge) on your right; on reaching the lane and Otterton Park * turn left. Entering the village of Otterton *, turn left down Maunders Hill towards the Green. At church wall proceed either through the churchyard down to the main street or keep west of the church on tarred road. Turn left at the Green past the Mill and over the bridge, turning immediately onto river path on left. Follow river downstream past White Bridge to estuary and Lime Kiln car park. Follow path at top of beach to Marine Parade almost as far as the Octagon * (Fairlynch * is a little further on the right), then bear left along the beach path. Turn right at the toilets, then left at the High Street. At the traffic lights turn right to the Public Hall.

* *See places of interest p. 4–8*

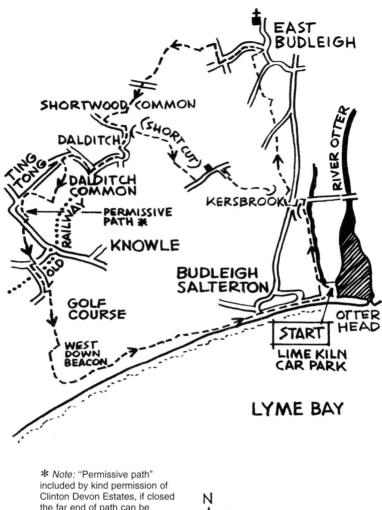

EAST BUDLEIGH

SHORTWOOD COMMON

DALDITCH

(SHORT CUT)

TING TONG

DALDITCH COMMON

KERSBROOK

RIVER OTTER

PERMISSIVE PATH ✳

OLD RAILWAY

KNOWLE

BUDLEIGH SALTERTON

OTTER HEAD

GOLF COURSE

START

LIME KILN CAR PARK

WEST DOWN BEACON

LYME BAY

✳ *Note:* "Permissive path" included by kind permission of Clinton Devon Estates, if closed the far end of path can be reached by road.

N

WALK 3

| KILOMETRES | 1 | 2 | 3 |
| MILES | 1 | | 2 |

16

3.

Budleigh Salterton; Kersbrook; East Budleigh; Shortwood Common; Ting Tong; West Down Beacon; Budleigh Salterton

A circular walk of about 7½ miles, mostly on fairly good tracks, with short distances on country lanes. The coast path gives some of the loveliest views in England.

Start from Lime Kiln car park, northwards on path behind SWW Pump House. Turn left at path T-junction and immediately right (public footpath sign to White Bridge). Continue up west side of Otter Valley to tarred road. Turn left along road to main (East Budleigh) road. Cross and turn right under disused railway bridge, then take left fork (Kersbrook ✽). After about 250 yards turn right (opposite "Rosa"). Continue up road which becomes a green lane. Cross tarred road diagonally and follow green lane to next tarred road. Turn right. A few yards down, turn left and follow green lane down to East Budleigh. Turn left almost immediately and follow track, between Wynard's Farm buildings until reaching staggered cross-track, where turn right and continue to stile on left. Cross and follow farm track to next stile. Cross, keeping to right hand edge of fields. Cross green lane by stiles on each side and continue along edge of field, and over next stile. Turn right along track at edge of Shortwood Common to T-junction with green lane, turning left.

(A short route back to Budleigh Salterton can be taken about 400 yards along this lane by turning left downhill between trees, following the last part of walk 4).

After ½ mile on the green lane, turn right down another green lane to tarred road at bottom. Turn right and follow tarred road. Take left fork at the small green opposite Dalditch Farm, and bear left again. After a few yards take narrow footpath half-left through trees and continue along east side of Dalditch Common, following broader track around south-west corner to lane at Ting Tong. Turn left along lane and shortly left over stile alongside gate into Leeford Plantations. Follow way-marked path to main road. Cross by stiles onto public footpath opposite. Follow track through woods to main Budleigh Salterton to Exmouth road. Cross with care and take the road opposite. Cross disused railway bridge and after 200 yards fork left onto footpath indicated by a metal sign to West Down Beacon, through a kissing gate. This track emerges onto the Golf Course.

Follow track alongside fairway (please give priority to golfers), turn right at junction and left at metal sign to West Down Beacon. At coast turn left and follow coast path to Budleigh Salterton.

✽ *See places of interest p. 4–8*

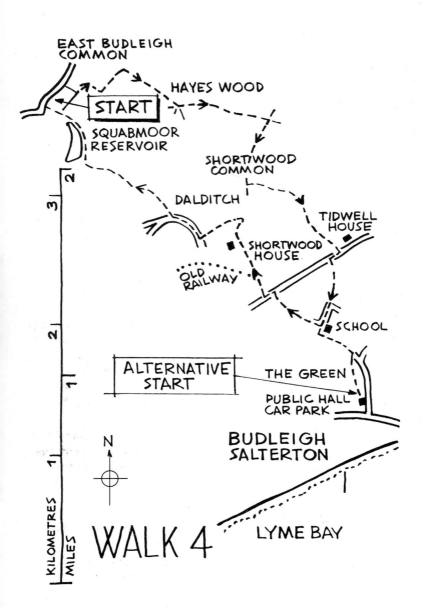

EAST BUDLEIGH
COMMON

HAYES WOOD

START

SQUABMOOR
RESERVOIR

SHORTWOOD
COMMON

DALDITCH

TIDWELL
HOUSE

SHORTWOOD
HOUSE

OLD
RAILWAY

SCHOOL

ALTERNATIVE
START

THE GREEN

PUBLIC HALL
CAR PARK

BUDLEIGH
SALTERTON

N

WALK 4

LYME BAY

KILOMETRES
MILES

3

2

2

1

1

18

4. East Budleigh Common; Shortwood Common; Tidwell; Dalditch; East Budleigh Common

A pleasant walk of 5 miles with very varied scenery. Muddy tracks when wet.

(Alternative start from Budleigh Salterton. From Public Hall car park walk up the Green. Turn left up Moor Lane into Bedlands Lane (school on right). Then continue from ‡ below).

Cross car park on East Budleigh Common (see p. 9) to Squabmoor Reservoir sign, turn left parallel to trench marking edge of car park. Very soon, where the path bends right, turn left and follow curving path to T-junction. Turn right onto this path. Take a left fork shortly before a fairly broad crossing path. Turn left onto this. On reaching another wide crossing at T-junction turn right.

Ignore a left fork leading down to a brick wall and descend to junction of tracks in dip, then take the lane straight ahead with woodland (Hayes Wood *) on your left.

Up gentle slope for 600 yards (Hayeswood Lane). At the crest there are stiles on each side. Cross the stile on the right and follow the left hand hedge to another stile. Across this stile take the centre grassy path and follow until a track leads off to the right down through trees (before grassy path turns to the left). Just before reaching a wider lane, you turn sharp left to follow a path downhill between the trees. (For those on Walk 3 this is the alternative route back).

Continue across 3 stiles, turning left towards farm and follow the path right of Tidwell House * to tarred road. Cross this with care. Turn right and in about 100 yards take first turning on left (Barn Lane) to St. Peter's School.

(If you started from Budleigh Salterton return via Moor Lane).

‡‡ Turn right into Bedlands Lane (‡). At the T-junction on main road, turn left and take lane on right (Bear Lane). Cross disused railway track and at Shortwood House go down track half right. Turn sharp left at bend and go downhill to tarred road. Turn right to Dalditch.

Leave the tarred road at junction, keep straight ahead through gate and follow a good stony track onto Common. Take two left hand forks and follow track downhill to Squabmoor Reservoir.

Continue along path on right hand side of reservoir beyond its head to a fairly wide path which converges from the right. Turn left onto this and then shortly turn off right onto a narrow path which leads back to the car park visible as a stand of mature pines.

* *See places of interest p. 4–8*

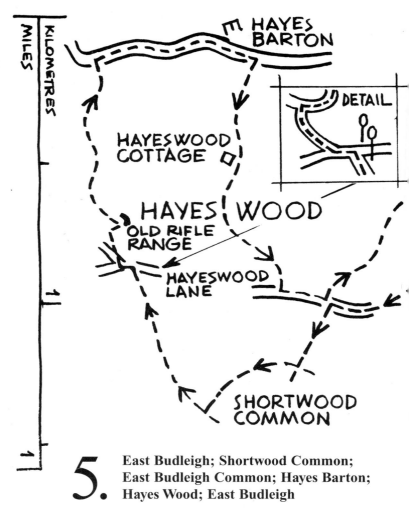

5.

East Budleigh; Shortwood Common; East Budleigh Common; Hayes Barton; Hayes Wood; East Budleigh

An easy walk of 4½ miles in delightful Raleigh Country. The lower places are muddy in wet weather. Start in East Budleigh Village car park.

The car park is just below East Budleigh Church✳. Turn right into Hayes Lane, passing Vicar's Mead✳. After 500 yards, turn left up track (Lillage Lane) facing electricity sub-station. Up gentle slope and down again (ignore footpath on right) to crooked cross paths: turn sharp right up track (Hayeswood Lane) for half a mile. At the crest of this track, watch for a crossing footpath (stile on either side) and take

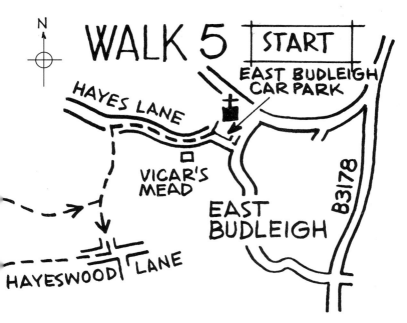

left stile; continue on field path with hedge on left to another stile, cross this to reach Shortwood Common. Lovely views. Turn immediately right over Common to a good track downhill to a T-junction; turn right down the track (Shortwood Lane) and after a left turn at a T (Hayeswood Lane), bear right at track junctions and follow main track to top of rise. Turn right at T-junction down to red-brick wall of a rifle range (relic of the 1939–45 War).

Continue on a good track with fencing of private woodland (Hayes Wood∗) on right, eventually reaching tarred road. Turn right. Hayes Barton∗, a 12th century farmhouse, will shortly appear on left. In about 100 yards, turn right up farm track, passing Hayes Wood Cottage, bear right and then left. Follow the signs through wood, ignoring a cross track, and at a T-junction (Hayeswood Lane) turn left. Proceed uphill to crest of hill, reaching the crossing footpath with two stiles, one on each side. Take left stile, following hedge on left, across fields with Hayes Wood above on your left. Magnificent views of Lyme Bay. The path gradually bears right downhill to a field gate leading onto a farm track, and eventually into Lillage Lane. Turn left and proceed to electricity sub-station, then turn right on tarred road and thus return to East Budleigh Church.

∗ *See places of interest p. 4–8*

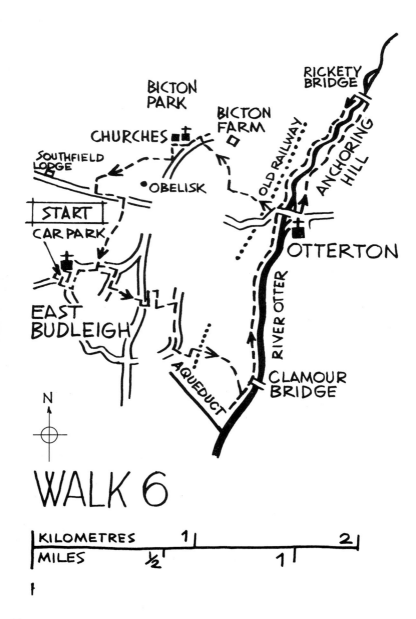

RICKETY
BRIDGE

BICTON
PARK

BICTON
FARM

CHURCHES

SOUTHFIELD
LODGE

OLD RAILWAY

ANCHORING
HILL

OBELISK

START

CAR PARK

OTTERTON

EAST
BUDLEIGH

RIVER OTTER

AQUEDUCT

CLAMOUR
BRIDGE

N

WALK 6

| KILOMETRES | 1 | | 2 |
| MILES | ½ | 1 | |

6. East Budleigh; River Otter; Otterton; Bicton; East Budleigh

An easy circular level walk of $4\frac{1}{2}$ miles, with much of interest en route.

From car park, just below East Budleigh Church*, turn left into Hayes Lane, and left again at High Street. Right into Vicarage Road, and after 300 yards right into Middletown Lane. After 100 yards cross stile on left into field, continuing by hedge and over stile to reach B3178. Cross this busy road with care, and turn right up the greensward and over a stile. Turn left and follow the path along three sides of the field to a stile in the hedge on the left. Cross this and follow the hedge on the right downhill to Frogmore Road (surfaced). Turn right, and after 400 yards, where road bends right, take lane on left. After a few yards climb steps on the left to the top of flood embankment; this soon bears left past sewage works. Cross disused railway track, following along embankment footpath across water meadows, to reach the river near footbridge (Clamour Bridge). Do not cross the footbridge, but walk upstream on west bank to Otterton* and there turn right to cross river bridge and reach The Green.

Halfway along The Green take footpath on your left between cottages; uphill over stile and along field path, for $\frac{1}{2}$ mile with river below on left, and Anchoring Hill* above on right. Turn left over a stile and cross footbridge (Rickety Bridge). Turn left again, and return to Otterton along river. On reaching main road, turn right for a few yards, and right again through a kissing gate onto a path with footbridges leading west. This path emerges, with Bicton farm on right, onto the B3178 almost opposite Bicton Park*.

Cross road with extreme care, turn left and in a few yards take path on right between stone walls, leading to Bicton Churches*. Turn left still between the stone walls, to reach a crossing bridle path (noting Obelisk* ahead); turn right under a line of trees and walk for about $\frac{1}{4}$ mile, with Bicton Park on right, skirting left around an enclosure and sheds. At the far end of the line of trees pass through line of hedge and turn left to reach a stile on the road. Turn left on the road, and in about 200 yards climb steps on the right and cross a stile. Follow the field path ahead into public recreation fields, keep to right-hand side to reach Vicarage Road; turn right and then left at T, and first right back to the car park.

* See places of interest p. 4–8

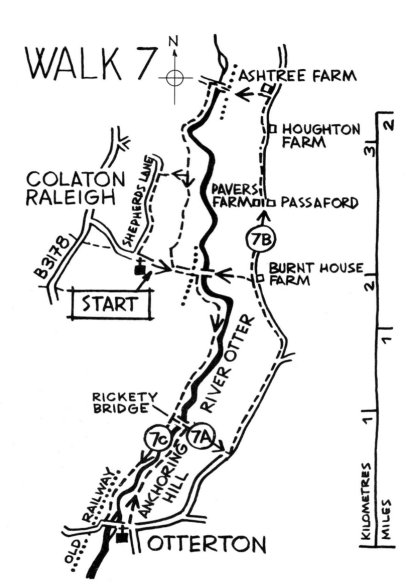

WALK 7

N

ASHTREE FARM

HOUGHTON FARM

COLATON RALEIGH

SHEPHERDS LANE

PAVERS FARM

PASSAFORD

B3178

7B

START

BURNT HOUSE FARM

RIVER OTTER

RICKETY BRIDGE

7C   7A

RAILWAY

ANCHORING HILL

OLD

OTTERTON

KILOMETRES

MILES

3   2

2

1   1

1

7.

Colaton Raleigh; River Otter; Otterton; Colaton Raleigh

A walk with three variations: A ($2\frac{3}{4}$ miles), B ($4\frac{1}{4}$ miles) with wide views of the Otter Valley, or C ($3\frac{1}{2}$ miles) which could include a stroll around Otterton – a fine example of an Anglo-Saxon village with its working Mill where refreshments can be obtained.

From Colaton Raleigh Church * walk down Church Road, across disused railway track, through kissing gate. At footbridge follow path right keeping river on left and continue on west bank through fields to arched wooden footbridge (Rickety Bridge) on left.

7A. Cross footbridge and stile. Turn left on path to another stile. Follow track right (signposted Rydon Lane) between hedges, turning left on reaching tarred road, and keeping left at fork (Pinn Lane Corner Cross signposted 'Northmostown $1\frac{3}{4}$ miles').

At the first farm (Burnthouse) footpath to left goes through gate and steeply down into field (first section usually muddy). Cross the field west to footbridge over river which leads back to Church Road.

7B. As above to Burnthouse Farm but, keeping straight on along road (attractive glimpses of the Otter Valley on the left), passing Pavers Farm (left), Passaford (right) and Houghton Farm. In front of the next farm (Ash Tree Farm) turn left along track. This track crosses old railway line by bridge, and river by footbridge. At bottom of steps on west bank turn left and go along river to far end of field. Through kissing gate, and up track to another kissing gate into field. Keeping close to hedge on right pass through yet another kissing gate and proceed with hedge on left. Ahead the track leads to the river end of Church Road or right to Shepherds Lane which leads (turn left) to Church Road, emerging opposite the Village Hall to west of Church.

7C. Do not cross arched footbridge. Continue downstream through gate on to main road at bridge and turn left into Otterton.

The return can be made along the same route, or forward from Mill to Otterton Green, following signposted footpath between cottages. Path rises to stile into field. Follow left hedge with glimpses of river below left, and Anchoring Hill * above on right: over stile and, still following left hedge, take stile on left and cross footbridge over river. Turn upstream to Colaton Raleigh along west bank.

* *See places of interest p. 4–8*

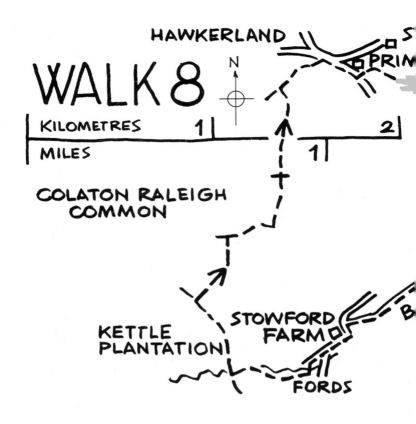

WALK 8

KILOMETRES	1
MILES	1

COLATON RALEIGH COMMON

KETTLE PLANTATION

STOWFORD FARM

FORDS

HAWKERLAND

8. Colaton Raleigh; Stowford; Colaton Raleigh Common; Hawkerland; Colaton Raleigh

A varied 5 mile walk over open country and Commons. Boots are advisable as there are patches that are always wet.

From Colaton Raleigh Church∗, west along Church Road, passing Village Hall (old village school) and an interesting thatched wall which conceals Place Court∗. Beyond the thatched wall go through kissing gate (left) between two bungalows, and follow footpath to Playing Field, then straight ahead along footpath emerging on B3178. Cross main road and leave it by opposite lane which climbs steeply for a few yards. At its T-junction with another lane keep straight on, along opposite track between hedges (Back Lane). Ignore a lane on right and, after crossing footbridge beside ford, turn left on road and continue past Stowford Farm on right. Keep to lane with

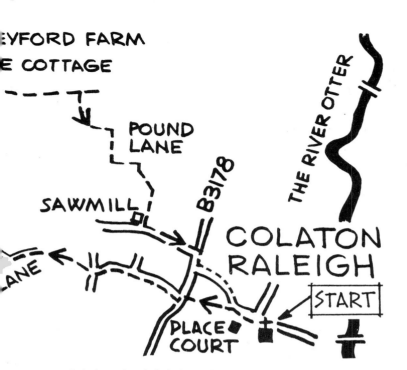

stream on left, ignoring left fork, and take broad track to right where the lane bears left (about 300 yards).

After crossing stream turn right up track between woodland on left and fields on right. After two fields, there is a small copse on right. Turn right through trees. After 150 yards veer to the left onto a narrow pebbly path running parallel with edge of the Common. Cross bog on low plank walkway. Continue along edge of Common under trees to a T-junction. Turn right and continue to signposts, where path becomes a broad farm track. Turn left and carry on, across a bog and narrow stream. 100 yards on take next farm track to the left opposite a field entrance and climb uphill. Turn right at T-junction and follow track downhill, to reach the tarred road at Hawkerland: turn right here (signposted Colaton Raleigh). Just beyond Primrose Cottage turn left onto track (signed unmetalled road) and continue across intersection. After a dip and rise, take right fork leading to Hawkerland Road (about ¾ mile) with Sawmills on right. Turn left down Hawkerland Road, then right at junction with B3178 and shortly left back to Church.

* *See places of interest p. 4–8*

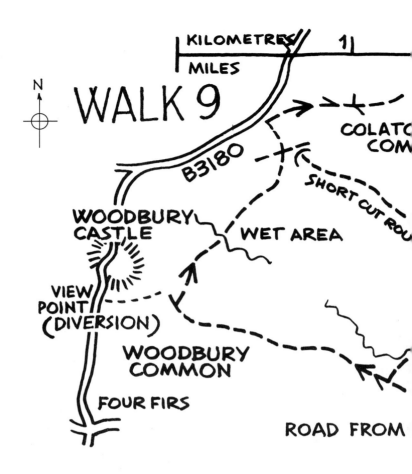

N

WALK 9

KILOMETRES / 1|

MILES

B3180

COLATO
COM

SHORT CUT ROU

WOODBURY
CASTLE

WET AREA

VIEW
POINT
(DIVERSION)

WOODBURY
COMMON

FOUR FIRS

ROAD FROM

9. Stowford; Woodbury Castle*; Colaton Raleigh Common; Stowford

Mainly over heathland, but some woodland. Very wet spots on the Commons, and a shallow stream to ford (boots essential). About 5 miles, (*with short cut 4 miles*). The short cut crosses a military range: do not cross if warning flags are flying. For advance information telephone (01392 873781).

From the car park at Stowford (see p. 9) turn left onto the road. Where the road bends right in a few yards fork left onto bridleway. Where the bridleway bends right, fork left through gate.

After the bridge across the stream turn right onto broad heathland track. From several places on this track Woodbury Castle* can be seen as a large clump of deciduous trees on the skyline, half right. At the T with a broad bridleway turn right. Ignore tracks on left and continue right.

Shortly before Woodbury Castle*, the main walk follows optionally the first or second of 2 broad tracks to the right. If you have time however for a diversion (about a mile there and back), go forward to the left of the Castle, over the road, and to the far end of the car park for a fine view of the Exe valley.

The main walk joins a line of trees south of Woodbury Castle. Where the line of trees bends left leave the trees and continue roughly straight ahead (NNE) down a path through a wet area towards a clump of pines on the skyline.

(For short cut, pass to the right of these pines. Several paths go right. The last of these, a right fork about 30 yards beyond the pines, starts short cut across Common (providing no warning flags are flying) aiming slightly to the right of High Peak in far distance. Follow path back to car park).

To continue main walk go left round pines, and only yards before the road, right onto a broad track. Follow this about a mile to the edge of the Common. Here turn sharp right away from the track, with hedge and agricultural land on your left.

At T with a farm track turn right, again with hedge and agricultural land on your left and the Common on your right. Where the track swings right veer left following the blue arrow. At T with a broad bridleway near a birch copse turn left to return to the car park.

✻ *See places of interest p. 4–8*

ELLIOTS FARM

VENN OTTERY
COMMON

VENN OTTERY

THE RIVER OTTER

BENCHAMS

SOUTHERTON

HARPFORD
COMMON

HARPFORD
BRIDGE

BROOKLANDS

HUNGER
HILL

CROSS

A3052

START

NEWTON
POPPLEFORD

N

WALK 10

KILOMETRES

MILES

3

2

2

1

1

10.

Newton Poppleford; Benchams; Venn Ottery Church; Southerton; Newton Poppleford

This 4½ mile walk has constantly changing views, a very interesting turning point at Venn Ottery Church, leading to the peace and quiet of Southerton. Some mud after rain.

Leave the car park by the path alongside Church and Village Green. Turn left at bus shelter along High Street. Opposite the Cannon Inn take footpath (No. 5) across Back Brook and turn left along path with fenced gardens on right. Pass through three kissing gates (in two fields) and turn right into Venn Ottery Road. Take second turning left (opposite Back Lane) up Hunger Hill and at grassy triangle fork right (Footpath 24) passing R.S.P.B. reserve sign. Good views.

Cross Harpford Common passing a large house, "Benchams", and a thatched cottage on right. Go ahead for 300 yards, then proceed up tarred road. At a copse turn right (signed "unmetalled road"). Wonderful views before bearing right downhill. Proceed (if road flooded, go through field alongside keeping close to hedge) then take green lane on left. Turn right on tarred road past Elliots Farm then right into path to Venn Ottery Church∗.

Leave churchyard by small gate (opposite South Door), bear right across village green to tarred road and, with new houses on right, turn left at large cottage, "Wayside". Proceed to T-junction at Southerton. Turn right then left at Spring Bank Cottage, left again at letter box. In 100 yards turn right (Footpath 23), across field to next lane. Proceed left along this lane to Brooklands Cross, half left to a field gate on Footpath 16 (East Devon Way). Follow purple waymarks uphill, pass down through first of two orchards turning right at bottom (Footpath 28) to pass through fields and kissing gate to Back Lane.

Cross lane, pass through Meadow Way Estate, turn left up steps, turn right uphill; left at High Street and right up the path alongside the Church back to Car Park.

∗ *See places of interest p. 4–8*

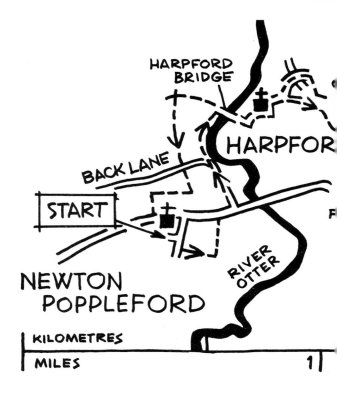

HARPFORD BRIDGE

HARPFOR

BACK LANE

START

NEWTON POPPLEFORD

RIVER OTTER

KILOMETRES

MILES

1

11. Newton Poppleford; River Otter; Harpford Woods; Bowd; Newton Poppleford

A 4 mile walk, taking in a pleasant reach of the Otter, the attractive village of Harpford and the well-known charm of Harpford Woods. Two possibly wet patches after rain.

Leave the car park above Newton Poppleford Church＊ by normal car entry into School Lane. Turn right, and in 50 yards turn left down Glebelands; pleasant view of the valley of the Otter. At bottom continue down sloping walkway. Turn left and then right (15 yards) down slope and steps to footpath at back of houses. Turn left on footpath and keep forward to main road (A3052). Turn right for 100 yards, and then left into Back Lane. Keeping Playing Fields on your left, turn right (where road bends left) through kissing-gate (Footpath 19), and then turn left. Keeping close to the river, go through a second kissing-gate on right into field. Continue to footbridge over river and cross. On reaching the road turn left and

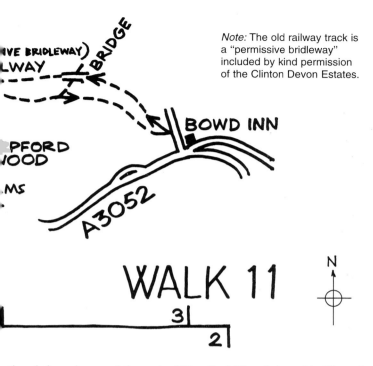

Note: The old railway track is a "permissive bridleway" included by kind permission of the Clinton Devon Estates.

BOWD INN

PFORD WOOD

MS

WALK 11

N

3
2

then left again round the end of Harpford Church ✳ and in 30 yards, turn right into Knapps Lane. In 50 yards, at bend by Littlecot House, turn right into Harpford Woods on Footpath 11. (At waymark post on left, stream on right, divert slightly to right to avoid muddy section).

Just past culvert and waterfall bear right along stream for ¼ mile. Over stile at barn conversions before lane at Bowd, turn back through gate and return by old railway track ("permissive bridleway", see note). After 1 mile turn off this track up to the bridge to cross left down into Harpford Village. Retrace steps around Church and past Village Hall. Turn right (Footpath 16) and re-cross river footbridge. Continue forward across field, through kissing-gate, over two bridges into copse. Turn left up steps, then forward to tarred road. Cross road into Playing Fields and leave at the far right hand corner.

Continue alongside stream for 100 yards to Meadow Drive, turn left uphill, then left on main road. Cross road with care and go up footpath on right side of the Church to return to car park.

✳ *See places of interest p. 4–8*

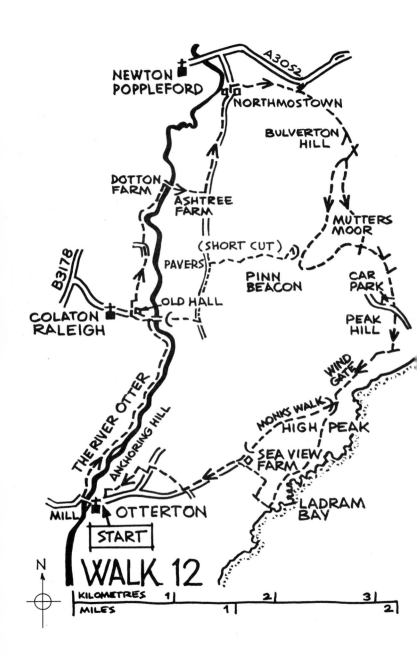

NEWTON
POPPLEFORD

NORTHMOSTOWN

A3052

BULVERTON
HILL

DOTTON
FARM

ASHTREE
FARM

MUTTERS
MOOR

(SHORT CUT)

PAVERS

PINN
BEACON

CAR
PARK

B3178

OLD HALL

COLATON
RALEIGH

PEAK
HILL

WIND
GATE

THE RIVER OTTER

ANCHORING HILL

MONKS WALK

HIGH PEAK

SEA VIEW
FARM

LADRAM
BAY

MILL

OTTERTON

START

N

WALK 12

KILOMETRES   1   2   3
MILES   1   2

12. Otterton; Colaton Raleigh; Bulverton Hill; Peak Hill; Otterton

A 9 mile walk which can be started from Otterton Green, Colaton Raleigh Church or Peak Hill (Muttersmoor) Car Park. The route given below starts from Otterton Green. The walk covers varied country, including riverside and field paths, a climb to Muttersmoor for some of the finest views over East Devon, (when the trees are cleared) and an interesting coastal and inland return route to Otterton. Muddy patches near Windgate may be avoided by an alternative path.

(Using the shortened route over Muttersmoor and via Bars Lane reduces the walk to 8 miles – The Colaton Raleigh cut-off cuts the walk to six miles).

From Otterton Green pass the Mill on left and cross over bridge. Through gate on right into field, follow path upstream through fields alongside river (1¼ miles) to footbridge at Colaton Raleigh.

(To shorten walk cross footbridge to tarred road, turn left for ¾ mile to Pavers, take track on right (signposted Mutters Moor) climb hill to rejoin walk at Pinn Beacon marked ‡ in text).

Turn left and cross disused railway track. Forward up Church Road to second house on right (Old Hall).

Immediately beyond Old Hall turn right up track and, in about ½ mile where track turns sharp left, go forward with hedge on right to kissing-gate. Pass through and follow left hedge to another kissing-gate opening onto a track leading down to a further kissing-gate into field by the river. Cross this field beside the river to footbridge on the right.

Cross the footbridge, follow track to Ash Tree Farm and turn left along tarred road. In about ¾ mile, just beyond Northmostown Farm✱, turn right on track (Back Lane). Follow this track uphill to a cross track immediately after a sharp left bend (about ½ mile). Turn right and in 70 yards fork right (signposted Bulverton Hill, Back Lane). Continue for about ½ mile and on reaching woodland take centre uphill track. At the top of the rise look back left to Keble's Seat✱, bear right on very broad track with coniferous woodlands on right. In a few yards the track divides. Left hand fork is direct route to Peak Hill car park. However for more varied views (again when trees are cleared) take right hand track, and after ¾ mile follow its sweeping U-turn to left. Then, when it turns sharp right, take the track straight ahead and eventually rejoin direct Peak Hill track from left.

✱ *See places of interest p. 4–8*

At car park cross the tarred road and follow footpath through gate and across first field; cross next field but bear right to forward hedge and, keeping this hedge on your left, follow coastal path west over two stiles; then left over stile marked with acorn (Windgate).

Where path widens at gate on left (signposted Ladram Bay) there is a choice of routes:

(To shorten the walk but missing fine sea views, continue forward down track known as Bars Lane (or the Monks Walk ∗) to Sea View Farm on left at junction with road; then proceed as from ‡ below).

Go through gate and follow coastal path to Ladram Bay (caravans), where turn right on slipway, and right again at telephone kiosk, following rough tarred lane to Sea View Farm. Bear left at ‡ farm. (‡) Forward by road (known as Higher Larderham Lane) for about ½ mile and a few yards past a left turn, go through kissing-gate on right, across a small field to rough bank and through a gate to field. Keeping to hedge on left descend to corner of field and on down enclosed track to road. Left on road, then right at 30 mph sign (Bus turning bay) to track in front of cottage, bearing left to stile into field. Half way across field pass through a gap in hedge, turn right and descend through field to lower corner. Over stile to an enclosed path leading down to the King's Arms Inn. Turn right for Otterton Green.

∗ *See places of interest p. 4–8*

∗   ∗   ∗   ∗   ∗

PLEASE OBSERVE THE COUNTRY CODE

Enjoy the countryside and respect its life and work.
Guard against all risk of fire.
Fasten gates.
Keep dogs under control.
Keep to public paths across farmland.
Use gates and stiles; avoid damaging fences, hedges and walls.
Leave livestock, crops and machinery alone.
Leave no litter – take it home!
Help to keep all water clean.
Protect wildlife, plants and trees.
Take special care on country roads.
Make as little noise as you can.